Dedication

Moaz Safi Yousef al-Kasasbeh
May 29, 1988–January 3, 2015

Also by Yatir Nitzany

Conversational Portuguese Quick and Easy

....

Conversational Spanish Quick and Easy

....

Conversational Italian Quick and Easy

....

Conversational French Quick and Easy

....

Conversational German Quick and Easy

....

Conversational Russian Quick and Easy

....

Conversational Polish Quick and Easy

....

Conversational Hebrew Quick and Easy

....

Conversational Yiddish Quick and Easy

....

Conversational Arabic Quick and Easy
Classical Arabic

....

Conversational Arabic Quick and Easy
Palestinian Dialect

....

Conversational Arabic Quick and Easy
Egyptian Dialect

....

Conversational Arabic Quick and Easy
Jordanian Dialect

....

Conversational Arabic Quick and Easy
Emirati Dialect

....

Conversational Arabic Quick and Easy
Iraqi Arabic

Conversational Arabic Quick and Easy

MOROCCAN DIALECT

YATIR NITZANY

ISBN-13: 978-1-951244-16-3
Printed in the United States of America

Foreword

About Myself

For many years I struggled to learn Spanish, and I still knew no more than about twenty words. Consequently, I was extremely frustrated. One day I stumbled upon this method as I was playing around with word combinations. Suddenly, I came to the realization that every language has a certain core group of words that are most commonly used and, simply by learning them, one could gain the ability to engage in quick and easy conversational Spanish.

I discovered which words those were, and I narrowed them down to three hundred and fifty that, once memorized, one could connect and create one's own sentences. The variations were and are infinite! By using this incredibly simple technique, I could converse at a proficient level and speak Spanish. Within a week, I astonished my Spanish-speaking friends with my newfound ability. The next semester I registered at my university for a Spanish language course, and I applied the same principles I had learned in that class (grammar, additional vocabulary, future and past tense, etc.) to those three hundred and fifty words I already had memorized, and immediately I felt as if I had grown wings and learned how to fly.

At the end of the semester, we took a class trip to San José, Costa Rica. I was like a fish in water, while the rest of my classmates were floundering and still struggling to converse. Throughout the following months, I again applied the same principle to other languages—French, Portuguese, Italian, and Arabic, all of which I now speak proficiently, thanks to this very simple technique.

This method is by far the fastest way to master quick and easy conversational language skills. There is no other technique that compares to my concept. It is effective, it worked for me, and it will work for you. Be consistent with my program, and you too will succeed the way I and many, many others have.

Contents

INTRODUCTION TO THE PROGRAM

People often dream about learning a foreign language, but usually they never do it. Some feel that they just won't be able to do it while others believe that they don't have the time. Whatever your reason is, it's time to set that aside. With my new method, you will have enough time, and you will not fail. You will actually learn how to speak the fundamentals of the language—fluently in as little as a few days. Of course, you won't speak perfect Moroccan dialect at first, but you will certainly gain significant proficiency. For example, if you travel to Morocco you will almost effortlessly be able engage in basic conversational communication with the locals in the present tense and you will no longer be intimidated by culture shock. It's time to relax. Learning a language is a valuable skill that connects people of multiple cultures around the world—and you now have the tools to join them.

How does my method work? I have taken twenty-seven of the most commonly used languages in the world and distilled from them the three hundred and fifty most frequently used words in any language. This process took three years of observation and research, and during that time, I determined which words I felt were most important for this method of basic conversational communication. In that time, I chose these words in such a way that they were structurally interrelated and that, when combined, form sentences. Thus, once you succeed in memorizing these words, you will be able to combine these words and form your own sentences. The words are spread over twenty pages. The words will also combine easily in sentences, for example, enabling you to ask simple questions, make basic statements, and obtain a rudimentary understanding of others' communications. I have also created Memorization Made Easy techniques for this program in order to help with the memorization of the vocabulary. Please see Reading and Pronunciation of Arabic accents in order to gain proficiency in the reading and pronunciation of the Arabic language prior to starting this program.

My book is mainly intended for basic present tense vocal communication, meaning anyone can easily use it to "get by" linguistically while visiting a foreign country without learning the entire language. With practice, you will be 100 percent understandable to native speakers, which is your aim. One disclaimer: this is not a grammar book, though it does address minute and essential grammar rules. Therefore, understanding complex sentences with obscure words in Arabic is beyond the scope of this book.

People who have tried this method have been successful, and by the time you finish this book, you will understand and be understood in basic conversational Arabic. This is the best basis to learn not only the Arabic language but any language. This is an entirely revolutionary, no-fail concept, and your ability to combine the pieces of the "language puzzle" together will come with great ease, especially if you use this program prior to beginning an Arabic class.

THE MOROCCAN DIALECT

In Morocco, the most spoken language in daily life is Moroccan Darija or Moroccan Arabic, which is spoken by some 19 million people in the country. Modern Standard Arabic is used for official communications by the government and other public bodies but is not spoken socially. Moroccan Darija has a strong presence on television, social media, entertainment, cinema, and commercial advertising.

Darija is a language derived from a variety of Arabic dialects spoken in Morocco and belongs to the Maghrebi Arabic language continuum. It is mutually intelligible, to some extent, with Algerian Arabic and to a lesser extent with Tunisian Arabic. It shows a very strong historical and linguistic Berber, French, and Spanish influence.

Several of the Darija dialects belong to two genetically different groups: the pre-Hilalian and Hilalian dialects.

Pre-Hilalian dialects are a consequence of the early Arabization phases of the Maghreb, (which means West in Arabic and comprises much of the region of northern West Africa), from the 7th to the 12th centuries, concerning the main urban settlements, the harbors, the religious centers (zaouias), and the main trade routes.

Hilalian, or Bedouin, dialects were introduced to Morocco following the Hilalian Invasion. The origin of this language goes back to over 3000 years, being a singular evolution of the Punic language spoken by the Carthaginians under Amazigh influence. Moroccan Darija is characterized by a strong Amazigh stratum.

Spoken in: Morocco

MEMORIZATION MADE EASY

There is no doubt the three hundred and fifty words in my program are the required essentials in order to engage in quick and easy basic conversation in any foreign language. However, some people may experience difficulty in the memorization. For this reason, I created Memorization Made Easy. This memorization technique will make this program so simple and fun that it's unbelievable! I have spread the words over the following twenty pages. Each page contains a vocabulary table of ten to fifteen words. Below every vocabulary box, sentences are composed from the words on the page that you have just studied. This aids greatly in memorization. Once you succeed in memorizing the first page, then proceed to the second page. Upon completion of the second page, go back to the first and review. Then proceed to the third page. After memorizing the third, go back to the first and second and repeat. And so on. As you continue, begin to combine words and create your own sentences in your head. Every time you proceed to the following page, you will notice words from the previous pages will be present in those simple sentences as well, because repetition is one of the most crucial aspects in learning any foreign language. Upon completion of your twenty pages, congratulations, you have absorbed the required words and gained a basic, quick-and-easy proficiency and you should now be able to create your own sentences and say anything you wish in the Moroccan Arabic dialect. This is a crash course in conversational Arabic, and it works!

ARABIC PRONUNCIATIONS

PLEASE MASTER THE FOLLOWING PAGE IN ARABIC PRONUNCIATIONS PRIOR TO STARTING THE PROGRAM

Kha. For Middle Eastern languages including Arabic, Hebrew, Farsi, Pashto, Urdu, Hindi, etc., and also German, to properly pronounce the kh or ch is essential, for example, *Khaled* (a Muslim name) or *Chanukah* (a Jewish holiday) or *Nacht* ("night" in German). The best way to describe kh or ch is to say "ka" or "ha" while at the same time putting your tongue at the back of your throat and blowing air. It's pronounced similarly to the sound that you make when clearing your throat. Please remember this whenever you come across any word containing a kh in this program.

Ghayin. The Arabic gh is equivalent to the "g" in English, but its pronunciation more closely resembles the French "r," rather than "g." Pronounce it at the back of your throat. The sound is equivalent to what you would make when gargling water. Gha is pronounced more as "rha," rather than as "ga." *Ghada* is pronounced as "rhada." In this program, the symbol for *ghayin* is gh, so keep your eyes peeled.

Aayin is pronounced as a'a, pronounced deep at the back of your throat. Rather similar to the sound one would make when gagging. In the program, the symbol for *aayin* is *a'a, u'u, o'o,* or *i'i.*

Ha is pronounced as "ha." Pronunciation takes place deep at the back of your throat, and for correct pronunciation, one must constrict the back of the throat and exhale air while simultaneously saying "ha." In the program, this strong h ("ha") is emphasized whenever *ha, ah, hi, he,* or *hu* is encountered.

NOTE TO THE READER

The purpose of this book is merely to enable you to communicate in the Moroccan Arabic dialect. In the program itself (pages 17-38) you may notice that the composition of some of those sentences might sound rather clumsy. This is intentional. These sentences were formulated in a specific way to serve two purposes: to facilitate the easy memorization of the vocabulary and to teach you how to combine the words in order to form your own sentences for quick and easy communication, rather than making complete literal sense in the English language. So keep in mind that this is not a phrase book!

As the title suggests, the sole purpose of this program is for conversational use only. It is based on the mirror translation technique. These sentences, as well as the translations are not incorrect, just a little clumsy. Latin languages, Semitic languages, and Anglo-Germanic languages, as well as a few others, are compatible with the mirror translation technique.

Many users say that this method surpasses any other known language learning technique that is currently out there on the market. Just stick with the program and you will achieve wonders!

Again, I wish to stress this program is by no means, shape, or form a phrase book! The sole purpose of this book is to give you a fundamental platform to enable you to connect certain words to become conversational. Please also read the "Introduction" and the "About Me" section prior to commencing the program.

In order to succeed with my method, please start on the very first page of the program and fully master one page at a time prior to proceeding to the next. Otherwise, you will overwhelm yourself and fail. Please do not skip pages, nor start from the middle of the book.

It is a myth that certain people are born with the talent to learn a language, and this book disproves that myth. With this method, anyone can learn a foreign language as long as he or she follows these explicit directions:

*** Memorize the vocabulary on each page**

*** Follow that memorization by using a notecard to cover the words you have just memorized and test yourself.**

*** Then read the sentences following that are created from the vocabulary bank that you just mastered.**

*** Once fully memorized, give yourself the green light to proceed to the next page.**

Again, if you proceed to the following page without mastering the previous, you are guaranteed to gain nothing from this book. If you follow the prescribed steps, you will realize just how effective and simplistic this method is.

The Program

Let's Begin! "Vocabulary" (Memorize the Vocabulary)

I | I am - Ana
With you – (Masc) Ana ma'ak / **(Masc/Fem)** Ana m'ak
With him / with her – (M) Ana m'ah / ana m'aha
With us - M'ana
For you - (M/F) Dyalk
Without him –Bla bih
Without them –Bla bihom
Always - Dima
Was – Kan
This, this is, it's – (M) Hada, had **(F)** hadi, had
Sometimes - Ba'ad lmarrat
Maybe –Yimken
You / you are / – (M) nta (F) nti
You (plural) - Ntouma
Are you?, is he?, is she? –Wash nta?/nti?, wash howa?, wash hiya?
Today – Lyom
Better – Hsan
He / he is - Huwa
She / she is –Hiya
From –Men

This is for you
(M) Hada dyalk (F) Hadi dyalk
I am from Morocco
Ana men lmaghrib
Are you from Casablanca?
Wash nta men Cazablanka?
I am with you
Ana m'ak
Sometimes you are with us at the mall
Ba'ad lmarrat nta m'ana f l mall
I am always with her
Ana dima m'aha
Are you without them today?
Wash nta/nti bla bihom lyom?
Sometimes I am with him
Ba'ad lmarrat ana m'ah

*In Arabic with the question "is it?", *wash* the "it" can pertain to either a masculine or feminine noun. However, whenever pertaining to a masculine or feminine noun, it will become *wash houwa* or *wash hiya*. For example, when referring to a feminine noun such as tonobil ("the car), "is it (the car in question) here?" / *Wash hiya hna?* When referring to a masculine noun such as *kelb* ("a dog), "is it (the dog in question) on the table?" *Wesh houwa foq tabla?* However, I yet again wish to stress that this isn't a grammar book!

I was - Kont
To be - (M) Ykun / **(F)** Tkun
The – El
Same – Bhal bhal / kif kif
Good - Mzyan
Here - Hna
Very - Bezaaf
And - W
Between - Bin
Now – Daba
Later / after / afterwards - Men ba'ad / ba'ad
If - Ila
Yes – Ah
To – L/tal
Tomorrow – Ghedda
You - (M) Nta / **(F)** nti
Also / too / as well – Tahuwwa (m) ta hiya (f)
With them – M'ahum

If it's between now and later
Ila bin daba o men ba'ad
It's better tomorrow
Ghedda hssen
This is good as well
Hadchi tahuwwa mezyan
To be the same person
Ykoun nefss shakhs
Yes, you are very good
Nta mezyan bzaf
I was here with them
Kent hna m'ahom
You and I
Nta w ana
The same day
Nefss nhar

Me – (read footnote)
Ok – Wakha
Even if - Hatta ila
No - La
Worse - Khayb ktar
Where - Fin
Everything - Kolshi
Somewhere – Shi blassa
What - Shno
Almost - Taqriban
There - (M) Kayn / (F) Kayna / tmma

Afterwards is worse
Men ba'ad khayeb ktar
Even if I go now
Hatta ila mchit daba
Where is everything?
Fein kolshi?
Maybe somewhere
Yemken chi blassa
What? I am almost there
Shnu ana taqriban temma
Where are you?
Finek
Where is the airport?
Fin ja lmatar?

*"There" has two meanings, so it is *kayna* or *tmma,* depending on the context. When we say "there is" we say *kayn* / but when we say "I am there" (place) we say *ana tmma.*

* *Fshi blassa* literally means "in a place."

*In Arabic, the pronoun "me" has several definitions. In relation to verbs, it's *liya. Liya* refers to any verb that relates to the action of doing something to someone or for someone.
For example, "tell me," "tell (to) me" / *(M) goul liya.*
'liya just means "me": "love me" / *ymoot 'liya*
Other variations *(ya)*:

* "on me" / *'liya*, "in me" / *fiya*
* "to me" / 'liya, "with me" / *maaya*

The same rule applies for "him" and "her"—both become suffixes: *–o* and *–a.* Basically all verbs pertinent to males end with *h*, and all pertinent to female end with ha.

* "love her" / *kanebgheeha*
* "love him" / *kanebgheeh*
* "love them" / *kanebgheehom*
* "love us" / *kanbghena*

Any verb that relates to doing someone to someone, for someone put *l:*

* "tell her" / *goolliha*
* "tell him" / *goollih*
* "tell them" / *qoollihoum*
* "tell us" / *goollina*

Adding you as a suffix in Arabic is *ak* or *lak,* female *ik* or *lik.*

* "love you" / *kanebgheek (M+F)*
* "tell you" / *qool-ek (M+F)*

House - Dar
In / at - Fe / be
Car – Tomobil
Already – Aslan
Good morning - sbah lkheir
How are you? – (M) Kidayr (F) Kidayra?
Where are you from? – (M) Mnein nta? **(F)** mnein nti?
Today - Lyom
Hello – Ahlan / Salam
What is your name? – (M) Chnu smitek (M+F)
How old are you? - Chehal f 'omrek? (M+F)
Son – Weld
Daughter - Bnt
To have – (M) 'Endo / (F) 'Endha
Doesn't - Ma… ash
Hard – S'eeb
Still – (M) Baqi / (F) baqa / (M+F) mazal
Then (or "so") – Men ba'ad/ ya'any / idan/ewa
In order to – Bash

She doesn't have a car, so maybe she is still at the house?
Ma'andhach tonobil idan tqdar tkun baqa f dar?
I am in the car already with your son and daughter
Ana aslan f tonobil maa weldek o bentek
Good morning, how are you today?
Ki dayer lyoum? Sbah lkhir
Hello, what is your name?
Ahlan/Salam, shenu smitak?
How old are you?
Sh-hal f 'omrak?
This is very hard, but it's not impossible
Hadchi s'eeb bzaf walakin mashi moustahil
Then where are you from?
Ewa mnin nta (M) Ewa mnin nti (F)

*In Arabic, possessive pronouns become suffixes to the noun. For example, in the translation for "your," *ak* is the masculine form, and *ik* is the feminine form.
- "your book" / Ktabek (M+F)
- "your house" / Darek (M+F)

*In Moroccan Arabic, *ka* is used to indicate cases of "to" or "to be able to." You will notice in the program that *ka* will quite often become a prefix to the verb "I want to learn," ana baghi net'allem or "to be able to go," *tkun qader tmchi.*

Thank you - Shukran
For - Dyal
Anything - Ay haja
That / That is – (F) Dik / (M) dak
Time - Mudda (duration)/ sa'a (if asking about the clock)
But - Walakin
No / not - Mashy / la'
I am not - Ana mashy
Away - Be'id
Late - M'atl
Similar – Bhal bhal
Another/ other – (M) akhor/lakhor (F) akhra/ lokhra
Side – Jnb
Until - Htta l
Yesterday – Lbareh
Without us – Bla bina
Since – Mlli
Day - Youm
Before – Qbel

Thanks for everything
Shukran 'ela kolshi
It's almost time
hada teqriban lweqt
I am not here, I am away
Ana mashy hena, ana b'id
That is a similar house
Had dar bhalha
I am from the other side
Ana men jiha lokhra
But I was here until late yesterday
Walakin kent m'atel lbareh
I am not at the other house
Ana mashy fi dar lokhra

*In Moroccan Arabic, with negations such as "no," "not," "doesn't," "can't," and "don't," use either *mashy* or *la. La* is used to indicate cases such as "are you here" – *nta hena* – and you then reply "no," *la. Mashy* is used to indicate cases of "not," "doesn't," or "don't," for example: "I am not at the other house" is *ana machy f dar lokhra.* In some instances both cases of *la* and *mashy* may be used, for example; "can you come?" "No, I can't," *la.*

* In Moroccan Arabic, in the event that "doesn't" is used regarding negations of verbs, the following requirements must precede and follow *ma … ch/sh*, for example: "she doesn't have the beer" (The verb "have" is *aand) – heya ma'andhach elbeera.*

*In Moroccan Darija Arabic, there are three definitions for time:
* "time" / *mudda* refers to "era", "moment period," "duration of time."
* "time(s)" / *marra(t) / khatra(t)* refers to "occasion" or "frequency."
* "time" / *sa'a* references "hour," "what time is it?"

What time is it? - Chehal sa'a
I say / I am saying – Kangoul
I want Ana bghet/ bghet
Without you –Bla bik
Everywhere /wherever – F ay blassa
I go - Ka nemshy
With - Ma'
My – Dyalli
Cousin (paternal) - (M) Wld 'amy / (F) bnt 'amy / (P) (M) wlaad 'amy / (P)(F) banaat 'amy
Cousin (maternal) - (M) Wld khaly / (F) bnt khali / (P)(M) wlaad khaly / (P)(F) bnat khaly
I need - Khasny
Right now – Daba
Night – Lil
To see - Nshoof
Light – Ddo
Outside – Barra / 'ala barra
Without – Bla
Happy - Farhan
I see / I am seeing - Nshoof

I am saying no / I say no
Nqool la'
I want to see this today
Bghit nchouf hadchi lyoum
I am with you everywhere
Ana maak fin ma kan
I am happy without my cousins here
Ana Farhan bla wlad 'ammi hna
I need to be there at night
Khassni nkoun temma b lil
I see light outside
Kanchouf ddo 'ela barra
What time is it right now?
Shehal f sa'a daba?

*"Mine" / *dyali* is also a possessive pronoun. *Dyali* means "my" but also becomes a suffix to a noun. Nouns ending in a vowel end with *–teh.* Nouns ending with a consonant end with *–eh.* For example:

* "cousin" / *wld el 'amm*, "my cousin" / *wld 'ammy*
* "cup" / *kass*, "my cup" / *kassi*

For second and third person masculine noun, *ibin* ("son"), male (S) *ak, (P) kom)* and female (S) *ik, (P) kum*). "His" – *Ilo* / "hers" – *ila*, noun endings will be *o* (for male) and *a* (for female).

* "your son" / *weldek*, "your (plural) son" / *weldkoum*
* "his son" / *weldou*, "her son" / *weldha*
* "our son" / *weldna*, "their son" *weldhoum*

For second and third person feminine noun: "car" / *tonobil*

* "your car" / *tonobiltek*, "your (plural) car" / *tonobiltkoum*
* "his car" / *tonobilto*, "her car" / *tonobiltha*
* "our car" / *tonobiltna*, "their car" / *tonobilthoum*

***This *isn't* a phrase book! The purpose of this book is *solely* to provide you with the tools to create *your own* sentences!**

Place – Blasa
Easy – Sahel
To find - Telqa
To look for / to search – Qalleb 'ela
Near / Close – Qreb
To wait – Tsenna
To sell - (M) Ybee' / (F) tbee'
To use - Sta'mel
To know - T'aref
To decide – Qarrer
Between - Bin
Both – Bjouj / jouj
To – La (to indicate a noun), ka/kan (to indicate a verb)

This place it's easy to find
Had lblassa sahla telqa
I want to look for this next to the car
Bghit nqalleb 'ela hadshi hda tonobil
I am saying to wait until tomorrow
Kangol lik tsenna tal ghedda
This table is easy to sell
Had tabla sahel tba'
I want to use this
Bghit neste'mel hadshi
I need to know where is the house
Khassni ne'raf dar fin
I want to decide between both places
Bghit nkhtar bin jouj blayss

*In Moroccan Arabic, in the event that "doesn't" is used regarding negations of verbs, the following requirements must precede and follow ma … ch/sh, for example: "she doesn't have the beer" (The verb "have" is *aand*) – *heya ma'andhach elbeera.*

*In Moroccan Arabic, to indicate "to," either *l* or *ka/kan* may be used. *L* is placed preceding a noun. In a phrase such as "going to a place," for instance, *ka/kan* is used to precede a verb, or to indicate "in order to." In certain instances, both *ka/kan* and *l* may be used, for example: "in order to go to Casablanca," *bach nemchi l Casablanca.*

Because - Heet
To buy – Shry
They - Huma
Them | their – Huma
Bottle - Qar'a
Book – Ktab
Mine - Dyali
To understand – Tefhem
Problem - Mushkil
I do / I am doing - N'mel / kandir
Of - De
To look – Shoof
Myself – Rassi
Enough – Kaafi
Food / water - Makla / ma
Each/ every/ entire/ all – Koll
Hotel - Otel

I like this hotel because I want to look at the beach
'Jebni had l otel heet bghit nshuf l bhar
I want to buy a bottle of water
Bghit neshri qar'a del ma
I do this every day
Kandir hadshi kol nhar
Both of them have enough food
Bjujhum 'andhum lmakla kafya
That is the book, and that book is mine
Hada huwa lktab, o had lktab dyali
I need to understand the problem
Khassni nfhem lmushkil
I see the view of the city from the hotel
Kanchof lmandar dyal lmdina mn l otel
I do my homework today
Kandir wajibati lmanziliya kol nhar
My entire life (*all my life*)
Hyati kamla

*"Both of them" is *bjojhum*

I like - Kay'jebny
There is / There are – Kayen
Family / Parents - 'Aila / walidin
Why – 'Alash
To say – Goul
Something - She haja
To go – Nmshy / (M) yimshy / (F) timshy
Ready – Wajed
Soon – Qreb
To work – Nkhdem / (M) yikhdem / (F) tikhdim
Who – Shkoun
To know - 'Aref
That (conjunction) – Belli, wash

I like to be at my house with my parents
kay'jbni nkoun f dar m'aa walidiya
I want to know why I need to say something important
bghit ne'raf 'elash khassni ngoul chi haja mouhimma
I am there with him
Ana temma m'ah
I am busy, but I need to be ready soon
Ana mechghoul walakin khassni nkoun wajed qreb
I like to go to work
Kay'jebni nemshi nekhdem
Who is there?
Shkoun tmma?
I want to know if they are here, because I want to go outside
Bghit ne'raf wash houma hna hit baghi nkhrej 'ela berra
There are seven dolls
Kaynin seb'a dyal lmounikat
I need to know that it is a good idea
Khassni ne'raf wash hadi fikra mzyana

*In the last sentence, we use "that" as a conjunction (*wash*) and a demonstrative pronoun *(M) hada / (F) hadik*).

How much /how many – Besh-hal
To bring – Jib
With me – M'aya
Instead – Blast
Only – Gheir / ghi
When – Fuqash / imta
Or – Aw
I can / Can I – Nqdar / yimken leya
Were - Kano
Without me – Bla biya
Fast - Deghya
Slow – Bchwiya
Cold – Bared
Inside – L'dakhel
To eat – Kla
Hot – Skhoon
To Drive – Tsog

How much money do I need to bring with me?
Chehal dyal lflouss khassni njib ma'ya
Instead of this cake, I want that cake
F blast had lkika bghit had lkika
Only when you can
Ghi fash tqdar
They were without me yesterday
kanou bla biya lbareh
Do I need to drive the car fast or slow?
Khasni nsog tonobil b zerba wla bchwiya
It is cold inside the library
kayn lberd ldakhel fel mektaba
Yes, I like to eat this hot for my lunch
ah, kay'ejbeni nakol skhon fel ghda
I can work today
Neqdar nkhdem lyoum

*"Were" is *ykun*, but for "they were," is *kanu* "We were" is *konna.*

*"I can" and "can I?" is *yimkn lya.* "You can" or "can you?" is *yimkin leek?*

To answer – Redd / jaweb
To fly - Teer
Time / Times - Mrra / Mrrat
To travel – Safer
To learn - Net'allam / (M) yt'alam / (F) tet'alam
How – Kifash
To swim - N'oom / (M) y'oom / (F) t'oom
To practice – Ytrina
To play - L'aab
To leave – Tkhelli
Many /much /a lot - Kteer, bezaaf
I go to - Kanemshy
First - Luwl
World – 'Aalamm

I want to answer many questions
Bghit njawb bzaf dyal as'ila
I must fly to Dubai today
Ana khasny teer l Dubai lyom
I need to learn how to swim at the pool
Ana khassni net'allam n'oum fla pissine
I want to learn to play better tennis
Ana bghit nt'allem nl'ab hssen f tennis
I want to leave this here for you when I go to travel the world
Bghit nkhelli hadshi hna 'ela qblek fash nmchi nsafer f l'alam
Since the first time
Men lmerra lowla
The children are yours
Lwlad dyalek

*In Moroccan Darija Arabic, "to leave (something)" is *tkheli*. "To leave (a place)" is *tkhrej*.

- In Moroccan Darija Arabic, there are three definitions for time:
- "time" / *mudda* refers to "era", "moment period," "duration of time."
- "time(s)" / *marra(t) /khatra(t)* refers to "occasion" or "frequency."
- "time" / *sa'a* references "hour," "what time is it?"

***With the knowledge you've gained so far, now try to create your own sentences!**

Nobody / anyone – Ta wahed
Against - Dedd
Us – Hna
To visit - Yzoor
Mom / Mother – Oumm/mmi
To give – 'Aty
Which - Eshmen
To meet - Tlaqa
Someone – She wahed
Just - Gheir
To walk - Tmasha
Around – Hawl
Towards - Tijah
Than - Min
Nothing – Walu / hata haja / hata shi

Something is better than nothing
Shi haja hsan min walu
I am against him
Ana deddo
Is there anyone here?
Kayn shi hed hna
We go to visit my family each week
Kanmchiw bash nzoro l'a'ila kul simana
I need to give you something
Ana khasny a'tyk shi haja
Do you want to go meet someone?
Baghi temshi tlaqa chi wahed
I was here on Wednesdays as well
Hta larb'a kent hna
Do you do this every
Nta katdir hadshi kulla nhar
You need to walk around, but not towards the house
Khassek tmshi hawl, mashi f ttijah dar

*In Arabic, when using the pronoun "you" as a direct and indirect object pronoun (the person who is actually affected by the action that is being carried out) in relation to a verb, the pronoun "you" becomes a suffix to that verb. That suffix becomes *ak* (masc.) *ik* (fem.).

- "to give" / *a'teh*: "to give you" / *a'teek*
- "to tell" / *qool*: "to tell you" / *qoolak* (m.), *qoolik* (f.)
- "see you" / *nshoofak*: "to see you" (plural) / *nshoofkom (m+f)*

For third person male, add *o* and *on* for plural, for female add *a* and *on* for plural.

- "tell him" / *goolih*
- "tell her" / *gooliha*
- "see them" / *nshoofhom*
- "see us "/ *shoofna*

I have – 'Andy
Don't – Maddirch
Friend - Saheb
To borrow – Tsellef
To look like / resemble – Tban bhal
Like (preposition) **–** Bhal
Grandfather – Jidd
To want – Tebghi
To stay – Bqa
To continue - Stamer
Way – Treq
I don't - Makandirch
To show - Wary
To prepare – Tsayb
I am not going - Maghadish

Do you want to look like Salim
bghiti tban bhal salim
I want to borrow this book for my grandfather
bghit ntsellef had lktab mn 'and jeddi
I want to drive and to continue on this way to my house
bghit nsog o nkemmel f had treq tal dar
I have a friend there, that's why I want to stay in Marrakesh
andi sahbi temma, dakshi 'elash baghi nebqa f marrakch
I am not going to see anyone here
maghadi nchuf ta wahed hna
I need to show you how to prepare breakfast
khassni nwerrik kifash tsayb lftor
Why don't you have the book?
'elash ma'andeksh lktab?
That is incorrect, I don't need the car today
hadshi mashi sheh, mamehtajch tonobil lyoum

*In Moroccan Arabic the case of "you don't have" is *ma'andkch.*

To remember - 'Aql 'ala
Your - Ta'ek/dialek (M+F)
Number - Raqm
Hour - Sa'aa
Dark / darkness – Mdallem/dlam
About / on the - 'Ala
Grandmother - Jedda / my grandmother – Jeddaty
Five - Khamsa
Minute / minutes - Dqeeqa / dqayq
More – Ktar
To think – Fakker
To do – Deer
To come – Ajy
To hear - Sma'
Last – Akher

You need to remember my number
Nte khasak t'aql 'ala raqmy
This is the last hour of darkness
Hady akher sa'aa dial dlam
I want to come and to hear my grandmother speak Arabic
Bghit nji o nsme' jedda kathdar bel 'arbiya
I need to think more about this, and what to do
Khassni nfekker kter f hadshi, o chnu yddar
From here to there, it's only five minutes
Men hna l lheh, ghi khamssa dqayq
The school on the mountain
L madrasa f jbel

*In Moroccan Arabic *dial* means "for (someone)" or "for" (something)".

To leave - Nkhroj
Again - T'awed
Morocco - Lmaghrib
To take - Nakhod
To try - Jreb
To rent – Kra
Without her - Bla biha
We are – Hna
To turn off - Tfa
To ask – Suwal
To stop - Wqf
Permission - Edn

He needs to leave and rent a house at the beach
Khassou ymchi w ykri dar fel bhar
I want to take the test without her
Bghit ndowez lemtihan bla biha
We are here a long time
Hna hna mudda twela
I need to turn off the lights early tonight
Khasni ntfi dwaw bekri lyoum
We want to stop here
Bghina nhebssou hna
We are from Rabbat
Hna men rbat
The same building
Nefss l'imara
I want to ask permission to leave
Bghi ntleb l idn bash nmchi
I want to sleep
Bghit n'as

*Morocco is officially referred to as *al-mamleka al-maghrabiya* (literal meaning: "The Kingdom of Morocco").

To open – Ftah / yhell
A bit, a little, a little bit – Shwiya
To pay – Nkhales
Once again - Merra khra
There isn't/ there aren't – Makayn
Sister - Okht
To hope - Tmna
To live - 'Esh
Nice to meet you - Metsharfin
Name - Smya
Last name - Kniyya
To return – Rja'
Door - Baab

I need to open the door for my sister
Khasny nhell lbab l khty
I need to buy something
Khasny nshry she haja
I want to meet your sisters
Khasny netlaqa khwatatek
Nice to meet you, what is your name and your last name
Metsharfin, shenu smitak w knitek?
To hope for a little better
Tmna shwya hsan
I want to return from the United States and to live in Qatar without problems
Bghit nerje' men lmirikan o n'ish f Qatar bla mashakil
Why are you sad right now?
'Alash mqllaq deba?
There aren't any people here
Makaynch nass hna
There isn't enough time to go to Agadir today
Makaynsh lweqt lkafi bash tmshi l Agadir lyum

*In Moroccan Darija Arabic, regarding the verb "to meet," there are two separate cases to define this verb: *tjtame'* and *tlaqa*, depending of the context. To meet for business is *tjtame'*. To meet for getting acquainted is *tlaqa*. In the sentence, "Do you want to go meet someone?" (the sister, getting acquainted with her), it's *tlaqa*.

***This *isn't* a phrase book! The purpose of this book is *solely* to provide you with the tools to create *your own* sentences!**

To happen – Wqa'
To order – T'amer
To drink – Shrob
Excuse me - (M) Smah le / (F) semhi le
Child - (**M**) Weld, (**F**) Bint
Woman - Mra
To begin / to start - Bda
To finish - Saala
To help - 'Awen
To smoke - Kma
To love - Bgha / moot 'ala
To talk / to speak – Tkallam/ hdar

This must happen today
Hadshi khaso ywqa' l-yom
Excuse me, my child is here as well
Smah le, weldi hena tahuwwa
I love you
Kanbghek/kanmoot 'alik
I see you
Kanshufek
I need you at my side
Mehtajek jenbi
I need to begin soon to be able to finish at 3 o'clock in the afternoon
Khasny nebda bekri bash nkun qader nsali m'a tlata dyal le'chiya
I need help
Ana khasny 'awn
I don't want to smoke once again
Mabaghich nkmi merra khra
I want to learn how to speak Arabic
Bghit nt'allem kifash nhdar bel 'arbiya

*"To be able to" is *ka+verb*. For example, "To be able to learn" (learn is *net'allam*) – *ka net'allam.*

*In Moroccan Arabic to signify "love" we can either use moot *'ala* or *kanbghi.*

To read - Neqra
To write – Nekteb
To teach - T'allem
To close – Qfal / sedd
To choose - Khtar
To prefer - Tfaddel
To put - Hott
Less - Qal
Sun - Chemch
Month – Shhar
I talk – Tkalm / hdar
Exact – Bddabt

I need this book to learn how to read and write in Arabic because I want to teach in Egypt
Khasny had lektab bash nt'allem kifash neqra o nekteb bel 'arbiya hit bghit nqarri f misr
I want to close the door of the house
Bghit nsedd lbab dyal dar
I prefer to put the gift here
Kan-faddill hott el cadeaux hena
I want to pay less than you for the dinner
Bghit nkhalles qall mennek ela l'cha
I speak with the boy and the girl in French
Kanhdar m'a lweld o lbent bel fransawiya
There is sun outside today
Kayna chemch ela berra lyoum
Is it possible to know the exact date?
Momkin ne'raf tarikh bddabt?

* "For the" is *lel*
* "In" is *fel*
* **With the knowledge you've gained so far, now try to create your own sentences!**

To exchange (money) **–** Tsarraf
To call – N'ayet
Brother – Akh
Dad – 'Ab
To sit - Gles
Together – Ma'a
To change – Tghayyer / tbaddel
Of course - Tab'an
Welcome – Merhba
During - Khelal
Years - (S)'Aam/ **(P)** 'a'waam
Sky – Sema
Up – Foq
Down - Taht
Sorry – Smeh li
To follow - Tbaa'
To the - Le
Big - Kbir
New - Jdid
Never / ever - 'Omry ma
Him / Her - O / a *(read footnote)*

I don't want to exchange this money at the bank
Mabghitch nsarref had lflouss fel banka
I call my brother and my dad today
N'ayyet ela khoya o baba lyoum
Of course I can come to the theater, and I want to sit together with you and with your sister
Tb'an nqdar nji l massrah, w bghit ngles ma'ak nta w khtak
I need to go down to see your new house
Khasny nhbet lteht bash nshuf darek jdida
I can see the sky from the window
Nqdar nshuf sema men charjem
I am sorry, but he wants to follow her to the store
Smeh li, walakin baghi yetb'ha l lmahal
I don't want to see you again
Mabqitch baghi nshufek merra khra

*In Moroccan Darija dialect, brother is *akh,* and dad is *ab*. However, "my dad" is *baba/ lwalid* and "my brother" is *khooya*. "My sister" is *khtey*, and "my mother" is *mama/ lwalida*. For the possessive pronouns, her (h*a*) and him (*o*), both become suffixes to the verb or noun. Concerning nouns: her house / *darha,* his house / *daro*. Concerning cases regarding verbs, please see page 19.

To allow - Smah
To believe – 'Aamen
Morning – Sbaah
Except - Ma 'ada
To promise - Waa'ed
Good night - Layla sa'eeda
To recognize - T'araf
People - Naas
To move - Harrak
Far - B'eed
Different – Mekhtalef
Man – Rajel
To enter - Dkhal
To receive – Twssl b
Throughout - Khilal
Good evening – Mselkhir
Left / right - Lisar/limen

I need to allow him to go with us, he is a different man now
Ana khasny smah lo ymshy ma'na, huwa rajil mekhtlef deba
I believe everything except this
Ana m'amen b koll-shi ma 'ada hadshi
I promise to say good night to my parents each night
Ana wa'edt ngoul lwalidiya Leila sa'ida kul lila
The people from Jordan are very pleasant
Nass fel ordon driyfin bzaf
I need to find another hotel very quickly
Khasny nelqa otel akhor dghya
They need to receive a book for work
Khasshum ytwesslo b ktab ela qbel lkhedma
I see the sun in the morning
Kanshuf chemch f sbah
The house is on the right side of the street
Dar f limen dyal zenqa

To wish - Tmanna
Bad - Khayeb
To get - Yakhod
To forget - Nsa
Everybody / Everyone - Kolshi/koll wahed
Although - Wakha
To feel – Hess
Great – Mohim
Next (as in close, near) - Hda
Next (as in next year) - Jai
To like – Bgha
In front – Qoddam
Person - Shakhs
Behind - Mowra
Well – Hssen
Restaurant - Restora
Bathroom - Beit el maa / twalet
Goodbye - Besalama

I don't want to wish you anything bad
Mabghitch netmenna lik chi haja khayba
I must forget everybody from my past to feel well
Khasny nsa kulshi mn lmadi bash nhess hsen
I am next to the person behind you
Ana hda chakhs li mowrak
There is a great person in front of me
Kayn chakhss mouhimm qoddami
I say goodbye to my friends
Kangoul bslama l shabi
Where is the bathroom in the restaurant?
Fein twalet f restoraa?
She has to get a car before the next year
Khassha tchri tonobil qbel l'am jay
I like the house, but it is very small
'Ajbani dar, walakin sghera bzaf

**Hda* literally means "side." In Arabic, it refers to "next." *Hdaya* is "besides me" and *hdak* is "besides you."

To remove / to take out - Hayd / zuwl
Please - 'Afaak
Beautiful - (**M**)Zwin, (**F**)Zwina
To lift – Hzz
Include / Including – Shmel
Belong – Ntami
To hold - Shedd
To check – Shoof
Small - Sgheer
Real - Haqeeqy
Week - Simana
Size – Qyass
Even though - Wkha
Doesn't - Mashy
So (as in "then") **–** Ya'ny
So (as in "very") - Bezaaf
Price – Taman

She wants to remove this door please
Bagha thayyed had lbab 'afak
This doesn't belong here, I need to check again
Hadshi makayntamish l hna, khasny nshuf 'awttani
This week the weather was very beautiful
Had simana ljaw kan zwin bzaf
I need to know which is the real diamond
Khasny ne'raf finahiya diamond l-hqeeqya
We need to check the size of the house
Khasna nshufu qyass dyal ddar
I want to lift this, so you need to hold it high
Khassni nhezz hadi ya'ni khassek thezha lfoq
I can pay this even though that the price is expensive
Nqdar nkhalless hadshi wakha taman ghali
Including everything is this price correct?
Shmel kulshi, wash taman sheh?

Countries of the Middle East

Bouldan sharq l awsat

Lebanon - Lobnan
Syria – Sourya
Jordan – L'ordon
Saudi Arabia – Sa'oudiya
Israel /Palestine /West Bank - Isra'eel / filisteen/ diffa algharbiyya
Bahrain – L'bahrein
Yemen – L'yaman
Oman - 'Oman
United Arab Emirates – L'emarat al'arabya el-motaheda
Kuwait – Lkouwet
Iraq – L'iraq
Qatar - Qatar
Morocco - Lmaghrib
Algeria – L'jazayer
Libya - Leebya
Egypt –Missra
Tunisia – Tunes

Months

Months

January – Janvye
February – Fevrye
March – Mars
April – Avril
May - May
June – Jwin
July – Jwiye
August – Out
September – Semptembre
October - Oktobar
November – Novembre
December – Decembre

Days of the Week

Sunday - Lhadd
Monday - Tnin
Tuesday - Tlat
Wednesday - Larb'a
Thursday - Lkhmiss
Friday - Jem'a
Saturday – Sabt

Seasons

Spring – Rbee'
Summer - Seif
Autumn – Khreef
Winter - Shetta

Cardinal Directions

North - Shamaal
South - Janoob
East – Sharq
West - Gharb

Colors

Black - Khal
White - Byad
Gray – Gri
Red – Hmar
Blue - Zreq
Yellow - Sfar
Green - Khdar
Orange – Lemoony
Purple - Mov
Brown - Qahwi

Numbers

One - Wahed
Two - Juj
Three – Tlata
Four - Rb'aa
Five - Khamsa
Six – Stta
Seven - Sab'aa
Eight - Tmenya
Nine - Ts'oud
Ten - 'Ashra
Twenty - 'Eshreen
Thirty - Tlaten
Hundred – Mya
Thousand – Alf
Million – Mlyoun

CONCLUSION

Congratulations! You have completed all the tools needed to master the Arabic language, and I hope that this has been a valuable learning experience. Now you have sufficient communication skills to be confident enough to embark on a visit to the Kingdom of Morocco, impress your friends, and boost your resume so good luck.

This program is available in other languages as well, and it is my fervent hope that my language learning programs will be used for good, enabling people from all corners of the globe and from all cultures and religions to be able to communicate harmoniously. After memorizing the required three hundred and fifty words, please perform a daily five-minute exercise by creating sentences in your head using these words. This simple exercise will help you grasp conversational communications even more effectively. Also, once you memorize the vocabulary on each page, follow it by using a notecard to cover the words you have just memorized and test yourself and follow that by going back and using this same notecard technique on the pages you studied during the previous days. This repetition technique will assist you in mastering these words in order to provide you with the tools to create your own sentences.

Every day, use this notecard technique on the words that you have just studied.

Everything in life has a catch. The catch here is just consistency. If you just open the book, and after the first few pages of studying the program, you put it down, then you will not gain anything. However, if you consistently dedicate a half hour daily to studying, as well as reviewing what you have learned from previous days, then you will quickly realize why this method is the most effective technique ever created to become conversational in a foreign language. My technique works! For anyone who doubts this technique, all I can say is that it has worked for me and hundreds of others.

Note from the Author

Thank you for your interest in my work. I encourage you to share your overall experience of this book by posting a review. Your review can make a difference! Please feel free to describe how you benefited from my method or provide creative feedback on how I can improve this program. I am constantly seeking ways to enhance the quality of this product, based on personal testimonials and suggestions from individuals like you.

Thanks and best of luck,

Yatir Nitzany

Lightning Source UK Ltd.
Milton Keynes UK
UKHW022213080420
361517UK00005B/461

9 781951 244163